"Bullied, Bungled and Botched"

by D. M. Larson

Monologues about bullying and depression.

Dedicated to the drama students
of Reynolds High School

For permission to perform these monologues,
contact doug@freedrama.net
(please include the title of the monologue in your request).

TABLE OF CONTENTS

SCENE 1 - BUG-EYED CREATURE (LUKE)............................... 3
SCENE 2 - CARRY A STUFFY (LAYLA)........................... 5
SCENE 3 - CALL ME DUMPER (LANE)........................ 6
SCENE 4 - PUNCH BOY (BING) 7
SCENE 5 - NO WITNESSES (MOIRA) 8
SCENE 6 - THE MUMMY GIRL (JANEY) 9
SCENE 7 - ODE TO THE SQUISHED (MR. DAVIS) 10
SCENE 8 - PROTECTO (KID HERO) (LUKE) 11
SCENE 9 - MAGICAL RAINBOWS (LAYLA) 12
SCENE 10 - A SONG FOR GRANDMA (BING) 13
SCENE 11 - FOREVER TREE (JANEY) 15
SCENE 12 - CUT OFF FROM THE WORLD (MOIRA) 16
SCENE 13 - TEACHERS EAT THEIR YOUNG (MR. DAVIS) 17
SCENE 14 - WHO WANTS TO BE MY BULLY? (LUKE) 18
SCENE 15 - PARENTING 101 (BING) 19
SCENE 16 - EMPTY BUCKETS (LANE) 20
SCENE 17 - GOOD FOR EACH OTHER (LAYLA) 21
SCENE 18 - FORGET ABOUT ME (MOIRA) 22
SCENE 19 - MYSTICAL EYES (BING) 24
SCENE 20 - ONLY CHILDREN BELIEVE IN BUTTERFLIES (JANEY) 27
SCENE 21 - SAFETY IN NUMBERS (MR. DAVIS) 36
SCENE 22 - END THE HURTING 37

BONUS MONOLOGUES

STRONG ENOUGH FOR BOTH OF US 38
TEARING ME APART 40
SHADOWS OF THE PAST 41
WISHING STAR 48
DOUBLE RAINBOW 49
MUCH MADNESS MONOLOGUE 50

SCENE 1 - BUG-EYED CREATURE (LUKE)

LUKE

Being the new kid at school is like discovering a new planet. Everything is strange and confusing and you're the weird alien everyone is afraid of - well not fear - you are the gross bugged eyes creature that's completely misunderstood.

(LUKE speaks like an alien to someone passing)

"I come in peace." Ignored as usual. Maybe I have on my cloaking device? No one seems to see me.

(He tries talking to more people as they pass and does the related hand motions for the following [ie Star Trek, Mork and Mindy])

Live long and prosper! Nano nano! Those are my geek gang signs.

May the force be with you. How come that one doesn't have a hand sign? It really needs one.

(He tries out different hand and arm motions)

May the force be with you... may the force be with you... may the force make you live long and prosper. I like that. I need to make a t-shirt with that on there.

You know, the principal made me change my shirt. I had one with Spock doing the Vulcan hand signs saying "Go Trek Yourself" Like anyone could be offended by that. He said students are not allowed to wear anything with words on it. Isn't that ironic? A school banning words.

School is not the place to be unique or stand out. They have this mold they want everyone to fit into. If you're not a certain way the whole school says you're not their type and they reject you.

Rejection - life is all about rejection. I am proud to say I have always been the last to be picked for any school activity. Especially when it's sports. I try to make sure I'm last - and if I am really lucky they have too many team members so I have so sit out. To make sure I am last to be picked I always limp so they think I am a liability - and if they don't notice the limp, I add in a nose pick because who wants to pass the ball to a nose picker? Oh, that's a good idea for a hand sign.

(LUKE picks his nose and holds out his finger)

May the force be with you.

(Laughs)

They noticed that one. I know that's gross but hey, I have my bug-eyed creature reputation to maintain.

END OF MONOLOGUE

SCENE 2 - CARRY A STUFFY (LAYLA)

LAYLA

I like to cuddle and hug. I loves stuffed animals. See. I have a new one. What should I name him? I think I will name him Mr. Cuddles.

(She gives the stuffed animal a big hug)

I have all these stuffies for a reason. I get anxiety attacks. I've had them since I was little. I used to scream a lot. Now I panic and can't breath. I don't even know what's scaring me most of the time. So I have to have these cute little guys and I hug the stuffing out of them. It's the only thing that seems to help - well, not always - today I had six anxiety attacks - that must be a new record.

It's the new school, all the new classes, all the new teachers. Why can't we just stay with the same teacher all day? I hate all this switching around - I'm a nervous wreck - I don't know what I'm doing.

So that's why I carry a stuffy. I need something to help me get through the day. Something to hold on to. I just wish they could hug me back.

END OF MONOLOGUE

SCENE 3 - CALL ME DUMPER (LANE)

LANE

They call me Dumper. I got the nickname when I was a youngin'... I was watching that Bambi movie. Every time I would see Thumper I would get so excited I would take a dump in my pants. I loved that rabbit for some reason. He just made me so happy. So happy I'd mess myself. We all need something like that in our lives. Something that makes us so happy we lose control. When ma finally got me potty trained, she didn't let me watch it anymore. So I had to find other things to make me happy. Not much did after that. No dolly or sweetie made me that excited. No boy could either. When I got old enough to like boys that is. They ain't worth nothing around here.

Boys here never could make me happy and I didn't want to make them happy the way they wanted me to.

I tried dating them some but it never works out. There ain't plenty more fish in this sea. These is shallow waters and there are pretty slim pickins. Seems like half of them are my cousins and I am not the kissing cousin type. And the ones left over after that are the catch and release kind. Because when you get one, you quickly want to throw them back.

So when I started breaking up with guys my nickname came back to haunt me. All the boys started calling me Dumper again.

That's the problem with a small town... things stick around from your childhood. You get a reputation and you get stuck with it. Everyone sees you one way and there's no way out. I could become the smartiest, prettiest girl in town and everyone would still call me Dumper. I could go off and feed African kids and cure Ebola and win the Nobel peace prize and come home and they'd still call me Dumper.

Why? Because it's easier I guess. Easier to keep you in your place. That way no one gets out of hand or too important. Know your place and play your part.

END OF MONOLOGUE

SCENE 4 - PUNCH BOY (BING)

BING

(BING is in a suit or tux standing by himself with two cups of punch in his hands)

It looks like Moira is having a great time. She looks so nice. I never thought such a pretty girl would want to go to the dance with me. I know I'm not ugly or weird or anything. But I never thought someone so beautiful would notice me.

It's been an amazing night. I rented a limo and she must have liked it because she did a million selfies so she could show her friends. She had me wear shades and open doors like I was her bodyguard. And I took her to this really fancy restaurant and she got a kick out of ordering the most expensive thing on the menu. Now she is dancing with her friends, having a wonderful time. She wants me over here, waiting, in case she needs anything. I'm holding her punch right now. I'm the official punch holder. Punch boy. Oh she's signaling me. She needs a drink. Coming right up, madam! She likes it when I act like her butler or something. It makes her laugh. I love that laugh of hers. And she and her friends laugh at me a lot.

END OF MONOLOGUE

SCENE 5 - NO WITNESSES (MOIRA)

MOIRA

I saw it... This terrible thing. It happened to this girl I don't even like. And no one knows who did it... Except me.

Do I tell? It's between what is right and what will ruin your life. I don't even like her... She brings it on herself. Why does she have to be so... Weird?

And if I tell... Everyone will turn against me... I will be like her... An outcast... Invisible. Is that how it happens... One little thing you do turns you into a leper? Social leprosy.

The right thing feels so wrong. I know I'm supposed to tell the truth but the truth will not set me free. The truth will ruin me... Keeping quiet will ruin her... And I don't know if I care.

I guess that's what happened to all those guys who stood up for what was right... Gandhi shot, MLK shot, Jesus crucified... I'm no Jesus.

I wonder if she could ever forgive me? She can get over it right? Forgive me... I don't want to be crucified.

END OF MONOLOGUE

SCENE 6 - THE MUMMY GIRL (JANEY)

JANEY
(Janey's face and hands are wrapped up in bandages)

This is me, the mummy girl. Mummy dearest. I want my mummy! I just had to get those jokes out of the way for you.

So... I'm sure you're wondering what happened to me. I'm telling everyone I got plastic surgery - but not to make myself more beautiful - I'm removing my nose cause everyone here stinks! I hate it here.

I have a pretty good reason for my bad attitude too. The kids here think they are so funny that they thought they'd push me face first through some glass. They wanted me to get a good look at their trophies in the big trophy case outside the principal's office. They think I'm jealous because I was staring at their trophies. They thought I was wishing I got a touchback or home down or whatever they call them. Or maybe they thought I wanted to be some bubble-headed cheer girl wanting to score with the guys. Oh, come on. Why else do they wear those short skirts?

Actually I was standing there and wondering why there can't be drama trophies - or charity trophies like best server in the soup kitchen. But no, the awards go to all the tight pants and short skirts. Bravo society! Bravo! Way to glorify the important things in life.

Beautiful people stink. That's why I want my nose removed. Their souls are rotten and I am tired of smelling their stench.

END OF MONOLOGUE

SCENE 7 - ODE TO THE SQUISHED (MR. DAVIS)

Through the wonders of evolution
A grasshopper learned to speak.

So excited by his revelation
The grasshopper rushed off
To tell the first human
He could find
About his amazing discovery.

But when the first human
Happened along
He did not see
The little grasshopper
Standing in the path
Waving his tiny arms...

And the careless human
Lost in his thoughts
Stepped on the poor little grasshopper.

And all he
Could manage to say to the human
Was "ouch"

END OF MONOLOGUE

SCENE 8 - PROTECTO (KID HERO) (LUKE)

LUKE

I've always dreamed of being a hero. I've tried everything to become super. I let a spider bite me... no spider powers; just lots of itching. I tried standing too close to the microwave oven hoping the radiation would change me. Nothing. And I got in trouble for making so many bags of popcorn. But I took it all to school and had a popcorn party. I was a hero that day. So I guess it kinda worked.

I love being a hero. I love helping people. I love making them happy. And I hate bad guys. I hate creeps who hurt people.

There's this kid at school... he is always hurting everyone. I am sick of him hurting us. I just need those super powers. I need something that will make him stop.

(Lost in thought)

Maybe if I eat more of the school lunches. They look radioactive. If I get enough green hotdogs and brown ketchup in me... something is bound to happen.

(Nods in approval)

And I need a catchphrase like "gonna smoosh me a baddie"... and a cool costume... actually last time I was in the bathroom, I saw the perfect superhero name. Protecto! Instead of a telephone booth like superman, I could use a bathroom stall and those Protecto seat covers could be a cape... and make a toilet paper mask. Nothing scares bad guys more than bathroom stuff.

(Thinks then frowns)

Or maybe it will really make them want to give me a swirly. I better rethink this.

END OF MONOLOGUE

SCENE 9 - MAGICAL RAINBOWS (LAYLA)

LAYLA

I live for rainbows. They are magical. I love how they surprise you.

They can happen anywhere and at any time.

Sometimes they're only there for a few seconds but I could watch them for hours.

And you know what's great about them ... Anyone can enjoy a rainbow... Rich, poor, famous, homeless, popular or loser.. Anyone can see them and dream.

The time they dazzle me the most is after a terrible storm. Lightening terrifies me but rainbows bring me comfort again.

There are so many stories about rainbows. You know like leprechauns and pots of gold. I'm embarrassed to admit this but when I was younger, I used to try and find the end of the rainbow. It's not that I'm greedy and want the pot of gold, I was just curious. But rainbows are mysterious and never stay in one place for long.

And then there's Noah ark - one of my favorite stories of all time - not only do you have rainbows but you have cute animals too. Ever notice how Noah only took all the cute ones? At least that's what you see in all the books and cartoons - super cute critters two by two climbing in to Noah canoe - and at the end, there is a rainbow- God's promise to Noah that he would never flood the world again. Although maybe we need another flood - or at least a good cleaning - some of the people around here could use a good holy bath.

Oh! Oh! Look! Lookie! It's a double rainbow!! It's really a double ray-ay-ay-bbbb-boooooow! Thank you rainbows! Thank you! I'm in Heaven.

END OF MONOLOGUE

SCENE 10 - A SONG FOR GRANDMA (BING)

(BING is singing the song "They Can't Take That Away From Me" by Billie Holiday)

BING
(Sings)

"The way you wear your hat
The way you sip your tea
The memory of all that
No, no they can't take that away from me"

(Smiles and speaks)

My grandma taught me all her old favorite tunes. She loved hearing me sing them. She said I am as good as any of those old time stars and way better than anything you hear today. She was always so nice to me. My grandma has been the most wonderful woman in my life. No one treated me better or made me feel more loved.

We'd spend hours singing together. She'd play the piano and teach me the words to all her songs. I loved it. I know it's weird. No one likes hanging out with old people. But my grandma never seemed old. She had such a young spirit. And see seemed so much more alive than anyone else I knew.

And no one knew me better. She could always tell when I was down or worried. She'd always listen and have the best advice. Even though Grandma never went to college, she was the smartest person I knew. I guess wise would be the right word for it. She was so much wiser than everyone else. She really understood life and had the answers. No one has answers anymore. Sure, people will listen but they don't really have any advice or know what to do. But Grandma knew. She always knew the the right thing to say that would help the most.

And now, I sing for her every day hoping she'll hear me in Heaven and send me a smile.

(Sings)

"The way your smile just beams
The way you sing off key
The way you haunt my dreams
No, no they can't take that away from me
We may never, never meet again
On the bumpy road to love
Still I'll always, always keep the memory of
The way you hold your knife
The way we danced till three
The way you changed my life
No, no they can't take that away from me
No, they can't take that away from me

We may never, never meet again
On that bumpy road to love
Still I'll always, always keep the memory of
The way you hold your knife
The way we danced till three
The way you change my life
No, no they can't take that away from me
No, they can't take that away from me."

(Smiles sadly and speaks)

They'll never take you away from me Grandma. You'll always be in my heart.

(Wipes away some tears)

Sorry about that. I'm a softy. Do you prefer something with a beat?

(Sings and dances as he leaves the stage)

"Hello my baby
Hello my honey
Hello my ragtime gal
Send me a kiss by wire
Baby my hearts on fire"

END OF MONOLOGUE

SCENE 11 - FOREVER TREE (JANEY)

(Janey still has some of her bandages on but you can see more of her face now and some scarring)

JANEY

Why can't everyone just leave me alone! They follow me after school and harass me - I go home and they harass me - maybe I need to stop shopping at Target. Because that's what I am. A target. People love to pick on me. The bullies have to take a number because I seem to be their favorite person to hate on. I'm some kind of stress reliever - they take out all their frustrations on me. I guess that is my purpose in life. At least I serve a purpose. It would be a shame if all that torture didn't have a purpose.

Then I go home and get harassed too. So I will just stay here behind this tree - forever. I love this tree. I do a lot of hiding behind this tree. I will even climb up and hide in the branches if I feel really scared. Sometimes I wish I'd fall out of the branches and break my neck. I dangle on a branch, begging myself to let go. But I'm never brave enough to do it. And I wouldn't want the tree to feel bad. This tree been good to me all these years. A quiet refuge on the border of madness and insanity. Safe from the madness of school and the insanity of home. I'm tempted to build a treehouse and stay here forever.

Or maybe I will lay in the middle of the road and get it over with. I'm tired of hiding. You want me? Come and get me! Finish me off. Put me out of my misery.

(The sound of a car approaching. She lies in the middle of the road [stage] - car sound stops and then sound of car honking. She yells at car)

Either run me over or go around because I'm not moving!

END OF MONOLOGUE

SCENE 12 - CUT OFF FROM THE WORLD (MOIRA)

MOIRA

Look at what they're saying about me! It's all over TwitFace! Everyone at school is seeing it. You see how many likes it's getting! I hate TwitFace! It's ruining my life! I can't go back to school tomorrow. I can't face everyone after what they said. What are you doing? Don't deactivate my account! Give me back my laptop! Stop, you're going to break it!

It broke. You broke my laptop.

Where's my phone? Give me my phone! Don't take out the battery. What are you doing with the battery! Put my phone back together! You're breaking it!

I'm cut off from the world...

(She cries and throws a tantrum. Then she stops and cries quietly. Then after a long pause she suddenly looks a little relieved)

I'm cut off from the world.

(Long pause - she looks around)

Wanna play a board game or something?

Hey look, we still have that tire swing in the back yard. Remember how we used to spin each other until we got so dizzy we couldn't walk? I loved that feeling. I wish I could feel that way again... not just dizzy, but... I don't know... carefree? Things get so much more complicated when you get older.

END OF MONOLOGUE

SCENE 13 - TEACHERS EAT THEIR YOUNG (MR. DAVIS)

You know what? Teachers eat their young. We're supposed to be these people who care about others and help people and make the world a better place, but we treat each other like crap. Some of the meanest people I know are here. They gossip and nit pick - and they stab you in the back. I have been stabbed in the back so many times I'm feeling like Julius Caesar. What's the point? This isn't even a business. We don't even profit from what we're doing. There's no advantage to "beating the competition" - what do we get out of destroying each other? Nothing - we're not promoted, we don't see huge raises, the people who work harder just get more work. This system is bogus and broken. We put so much into these kids who come and go and never see again - but we put nothing into each other - we don't invest anything in the people we see day after day - year after year - the ones who should build us up just tear us down.

Teachers eat their young - that's why most of us don't last very long and why the ones who do stay are so burned out. We become empty shells, zombies that wander the halls and look for brains to educate. And sometimes I wonder if we even do that.

When I was a kid, we used to give out warm fuzzies. They were these little notes we'd write in school that had to be nice things we thought about each other. The teachers did it too. That was a much nicer time. Sure, I know nobody likes that touchy feely self-esteem stuff anymore… but I miss it. I miss the warm fuzzies and miss knowing that someone cared.

END OF MONOLOGUE

SCENE 14 - WHO WANTS TO BE MY BULLY?
(LUKE)

LUKE

Hello. I am taking applications to my official bully. I want to make sure the right person is picking on me day after day. It's a very unique and special relationship. Ready for some questions? Okay. First of all, are you interested in my lunch money or my lunch? Because if you need the cash I will bring that it if you prefer to have me bring a lunch already prepared, I can do that too.

No this isn't a joke. I'm very serious about this. Or do you prefer I tell jokes? Are you the knock knock joke kind where you walk up and knock on my head? Knock! Knock! Or do you prefer the walk in to the bar kind of jokes?

I could try work up some dirty jokes too but that seems more appropriate for your friends to tell than your victims. We have to have the right kind of relationship here. We need familiarity without closeness.

I can provide services such as homework preparation and go-foring - in return I ask that I only receive swirlies at the end of the day so I can go home and shower after. And then one more thing - the most important part of all this - I ask for your protection. I want you to protect me from all the other bullies. This has to be an exclusive bullying arrangement and you have to make sure you step in at the first sign of any danger from other bullies. I like my day to be predictable - deliver your homework in the morning - lunch or lunch money at noon and then a farewell swirly or wedgie in the afternoon - yes I will even throw a few wedgies in the deal - so what do you say? Do we have a deal? Good - sign here please.

END OF MONOLOGUE

SCENE 15 - PARENTING 101 (BING)

BING

Welcome to Parenting 101. Lesson 1 - kill off his passion. We can't have him too excited about anything. And if he likes it too much there must be something wrong with it. So we must do everything in our power to discourage him. Little do they know it only makes me want it more.

It sucks when you don't fit in the place you spend your entire day. I feel so out of place at school.

But home isn't any better. My parents even homeschooled me for awhile. I guess they bullied me to give make the school experience as real as possible.
They were always fitting me for a dunce hat because I was never good enough at anything they wanted me to learn. But I was never able to walk on water or turn water into wine.

I wonder what I would have thought of my parents as teens? If we were all teens together. It would be interesting to go back in time and meet them, like a Back to the Future thing. I wonder what they were like. I want to see if they were liked or a loser like me.

They were probably popular. That's why they are so disappointed in me. If they were losers too, then they'd understand me more - understanding what I'm going through - and we could be friends.

END OF MONOLOGUE

SCENE 16 - EMPTY BUCKETS (LANE)

LANE

But why do I have to buy the buckets from you. Can't you just give them to me? But you got them for free. Who'd want to buy these? No one needs a bunch of old used cans! No I'm not upset!

(clearly is)

Fine. Here's my $20. The 20 I worked half the summer to get picking strawberries. Sorry I quit okay? It was killing my back. That's the toughest $20 of my life.

So I get 40 buckets... and I sell them for a dollar. I'll double my money. But what if I can't sell them?

(sarcastic)

Yeah, yeah. I know. No negative talk. I gotta visualize success.

(sees buckets)

Wait. You sold me dirty buckets? But you got them for free... AND you want me to clean them? What's in here? Tar?!

How do I scrub tar out of these? A wire brush. Oh this will be fun. I should have just sold lemonade. Can I? And lose my investment? You mean you won't give me my money back? But...I'm your kid. Why are you doing this to me?

You want me to learn a lesson. What lesson? That my dad is a crook?

END OF MONOLOGUE

SCENE 17 - GOOD FOR EACH OTHER (LAYLA)

LAYLA

Parents. They want to toughen us up but instead they tear us down. Why does being tough involve being mean to your kid?

I thought everyone was this way ...so many people in my life act this way - don't be a cry baby - don't be a wimp - quit being so sensitive - but then I found you.

But we build each other up - that's what makes us so good for each other.

And being sensitive doesn't seem so bad anymore - being sensitive means that I am more caring and more loving - how can that be bad? To them it is, but not to you. And that's why I'm falling in love.

END OF MONOLOGUE

SCENE 18 - FORGET ABOUT ME (MOIRA)

MOIRA

I suffer every day and you don't even see it. You don't see the hurt inside me do you? But it's too much to hold inside anymore.

I can't handle it... I'm going crazy. The fear is crippling me... I have to drag myself out of bed and force myself to live each day... Sure, I put on this happy face... I bet you think I am pretty cheerful... No one cares to see the pain under my skin... The pain that's ripping at me... And tearing me apart.

What's wrong with me? You sure you want to know?

I feel like I am never good enough for you.

(Anger builds)

No matter what I do it's not as good as my sister. I always have to hear how she would have done it better. Or how she already did it better.

(Hurt)

Why does she want to ruin my life? She just wants to blot me out like I was some sort of mistake... I'm just a copy... A copy of a copy... Not as good as the original... Not as good as you.

(Sarcastic and bitter)

You are so perfect... Everyone around me is so perfect... And there was nothing left over for me... I am the leftover failures... I am the fatty waste you toss to the dogs.

(Fury)

Everyone hates me! Why does everyone think I am so horrible...

(Shakes and tries to hold back the fury)

Probably because I am. A horrible creature doomed to walk this earth and suffer... For you.

(Cries uncontrollably... Struggles to speak)

I'm hurting... Hurting so bad inside. Cut off from everyone ... Punished for some past life wrongs... What did I do in a past life to deserve this?.. Or am I paying for the sins of my father... And mother... Am I your sin? Or do I remind you of some sin you want to forget?

(Anger builds)

Or I am a disappointment that keeps disappointing... I even disappoint myself.

(Furious)

I will never be my sister. I don't want to be her. I hate everything about her!

(Cries... Sadness)

But I don't want to be me either. Sometimes I want to fade away... Become a shadow... Fading away... Forgotten... Maybe if you forget about me I won't make you so sad anymore.

END OF MONOLOGUE

SCENE 19 - MYSTICAL EYES (BING)

(Bing is sitting by a museum display of a mummy sarcophagus of a young woman. Her belongings are in displays around her)

BING

I'm so glad I found you. You're the only one I can talk to. Definitely the only girl I've ever talked to. But I feel so comfortable with you.

No one listens to me. I talk. They change the subject. It's not that I feel like I have something better to say. I don't know if I have much to say at all. I've never had a chance to try.

But I found you... Here in this museum. Alone with no one to talk to. Like me. Like each other. Pushed back in a corner and forgotten. But we aren't alone anymore.

The minute I saw you here, I knew you were special. There was something magical about your eyes. I know they aren't your actual eyes, but the eyes they painted you... Mystical eyes that gazed upon me and held me here. Did the artist capture your true eyes? If so they are the most amazing ones I have ever seen.

You're so pretty. Such a beautiful princess... Didn't your people believe you were a goddess if you were royalty? I could worship you. I hope you don't mind me saying that.

What's it like to be worshiped? Not that I want to be. I imagine there are down sides. Like Princess Diana... Don't be jealous. I never met the woman... But she was killed by the people who loved her too much. I guess it possible to love something too much. Like Lenny and the rabbit... Hugging and squeezing the life out of what you love so much. I hope your people didn't do that to you.

It's important to love just enough. Just enough to know you are loved without hurting the object of your affection.

But you died so young. It's not fair. No one should have such a short life.

Egyptians believed in immortality or some such thing. You live on, remembered but no one to talk to. Never getting to say anything.

I guess I was a mummy before I met you. There ...but not being heard.

I wish I could give you what you've given me... A voice. A chance to exist. A chance to be real.

So much of life is fake. It would be wonderful to be real.. To be real together... A real life for the two of us.

What would we do first? Good question. What does one do for a princess?

Do princesses like picnics? I know a nice place where we could go. It's a meadow near a creek. The sound of water drowns out the world around you. You only hear the birds and the wind through the leaves. You watch the clouds and dream.

Did you ever watch the clouds and dream them into something? I create the most amazing pictures in the clouds. I would love to show you how.

I would teach you. Teach you the way to dream beautiful pictures in the sky.

What is my favorite dream? A Phoenix. Rising from the ashes and burning brighter than the sun.

Does it sound nice? You want to hear more? What else would we do?

We'd watch the sunset fires burn away the day and hold hands as the colors dazzle us and burn away the worries of today.

Then as the fire dies, the embers float above us and turn to stars.

The stars sparkling down on us like a crown worthy of a princess.

We'd get closer until I was holding you and then you'd fall asleep in my arms, but I couldn't sleep. I wouldn't want to miss any moment with you. Holding you, feeling your body close to my own... that would be better than any dream.

Would you like that? Me too. More than anything.

That's my wish. The wish for the princess of Giza.

Giza? That where you are from isn't it? Does that make you a geezer? Sorry. Couldn't resist.

I better go. What's that? A gift? You don't need to give me anything. Being with you is enough. I can't take your ring. Please don't cry. I would if I could but the museum... I know it's yours but...
Shh... it's alright... I will take it. Really, I will. Watch.

(He nervously looks around and crawls over a barrier. He carefully opens a container and is happy when an alarm doesn't go off. He picks up the ring and shows her)

This one? It's beautiful. Your fingers are so tiny. You must have the most beautiful hands.

(He crawls out of barrier and looks around, happy he didn't get caught)

I will cherish this. This means a lot to me. I've never been given anything by a girl before. I will keep it with me always so I can dream about you... Dream we were made for each other ... I for you and you saved for me. I love it...

(Steps away)

And I love you.

END OF MONOLOGUE

SCENE 20 - ONLY CHILDREN BELIEVE IN BUTTERFLIES (JANEY)

(Janey is in a garden watching the stars in the sky. She becomes upset when someone approaches)

JANEY

I was hoping I could be alone out here in the garden. No one ever comes here in the evening. I wanted to be here for the stars.

(Angrily)

I don't want anything - and I don't want to talk anymore - can I please be by myself? That's all you've done here - poke, prod, and pry - I've never felt so violated before - I just want to be left alone.

(Pause)

I don't like being around anyone. I get upset when I'm in a room full of people.

(Pause. afraid)

I get really scared - I almost feel like I can't breathe - I just need to be alone, Doctor - I know you don't really care - you're simply doing your job - once I'm "better" you'll be through with me - then it's on to another patient - you're just like anyone else -

(Almost shouting)

You probably haven't cared about any patient in years - that would be unprofessional - an unnecessary burden on your conscience - Please, just go - I know what I need better than you -

You're not God, you know - you don't have the powers to cure everything - I know what you can and can't do -Go on - get out of here!

(Pause - she gets an evil smile)

Relax?

(Laughs)

How can I relax with you bothering me all the time? If there's another way, I'd like to know how -

(Pause. Turns away)

Is there anything else you wish to pry out of me? No? Good - then goodnight -

(JANEY starts weeding the flower bed)

I thought you were leaving - Sorry but I'm busy - I'm killing weeds - Cultivating beauty by killing the ugly - it's an odd practice - in reality its weeds on which the soil feeds -

(Stops)

But few people find the truth as fulfilling - If only you had planted something more useful - beans, or tomatoes, then the sacrifice might be worthwhile - but flowers, they're more difficult to justify - Frail beauty - that's all they are - cultivated for weakness - and has very little nutritional value - in the end they never can satisfy - always a disappointment as they wither and die - Frail and weak - a light frost would snap its neck -

(JANEY breaks the head off a flower)

So easily smitten by one little insect -

(JANEY holds up broken bud to a weed)

The choice is so easy for most - Yet it's not - I suppose most people don't give it much thought -

(Looks up at sky)

I know a story of a man who had a plant which most called a useless weed - it turned out the weed was a cure for cancer - but the weed was nearly extinct so no one got the cure - do you believe in such a thing? Do you believe in anything?

(Pause)

Oh, never mind - I guess to you most beliefs are only fables -

(Throws both plants down - upset)

No one really cares, do they? They pay you to care - everywhere it's the same way - People should only fix what's broken - Why couldn't you all just leave me alone? Nothing was wrong with me before you found me - I was happy at home - alone - shut out from then world - protected -

(Pause. Calms a moment. Grows sadder)

I had to be alone - I - I needed to hide - I had no choice - I had to get away - I couldn't live like the others anymore -

(Angry)

Why do you want to know all this?

(Furious)

I said I don't want to talk anymore! Leave me alone! I don't have to tell you anything! I'm not a little kid.

(Bends over and buries her face in her hands)

There's so much you don't know - I just need to be alone - Why can't they leave me alone?

(She sees something)

But I'm never alone - There's always someone - Or something - Around me - Following me - They're always near - Spirits - Ghosts - Shadows of the past - Ghosts have always been with me. Not by choice. At least not on my part. It just happens. I don't want to believe... but they've forced themselves on me.

(Thoughtful)

Perhaps the old Indian woman did it to me. I lived in her house too long as a child.

(Looks at ceiling)

At night, footsteps paced the ceiling. Over and over, an impatient march, forever in step to a silent drum. If only this had been my only encounter, I could dismiss it. "The house is settling," my mother said... but this wasn't all the house did. Lights dimmed and glowed. Her ghostly will stronger than the new world magic conjured by GE. I slept in my room. Well, not really slept. Sleep was never something I did much of, especially early on. My worries at seven far outweighed my need for sleep. Awake. Forever awake. My father had left me. My mother... I was always worried mother would leave me too. I wish the ghosts would go. But they linger. Always lingering. Never really gone. The old Indian woman was my first. She rocked at my beside, all in white. My eyes met hers. Her eyes giving me a worried look as if I were the one who had expired. Fear making my head sink deeply into covers. My eyes entombed by my lids. How long she waited, I'll never know. By dawn I ventured a look. She was gone... or perhaps she was never there. Thinking the apparition a dream, I told my family and their eyes betrayed them. Others had known her too. Mother had a vision. She did not go questing for it though. The old Indian, young to most who saw her, once lived on this land. A servant. A girl died here, she at her side... at her side rocking... and the girl died. I wish I could have been there for her too... Spirits dog me. Just when I no longer believe, they appear. Flashing white lights. A cold touch. They return. Even now. But this time it was too much. Another place. Another spirit. This time it was someone I knew.

(Slowly turns to panic during following)

It started with the call. The news that she had gone away. Finding myself in tears. Tears sapping me dry. Would the tears ever stop? Pain like a thick metal pole shoved up your ass.

(Tries to calm herself but panics again)

I had lost everything. An emptiness replaced love, anxious to find, nothing there... no "body" anyway, but something. Something that opens doors, something leaving tissue by the bed. The dog barking at nothing... but something. Finding things in new places, things missing. The locked door... open.

(Tries to calm herself)

Explanations fly. Knowledge our protection.

(Thinks a moment. Frowns and shivers)

It began with the cold. Spots of cold. A moment of normal then cold, as if the heat were sucked into another dimension. These don't bother me as much as the touch. A handless touch of nothing. Something grabbed by arm but no one was there.

(Pulls back in fear and runs. She falls to the ground)

I ran for bed, buried myself in covers and waited for dawn.

(She curls up in a ball. Pause)

You're never too old to hide under the covers. Wrapping yourself up into a cocoon. Hoping that when you emerge life will be butterflies again.

(She sighs and sits up)

But only children believe in butterflies.

(She rises again)

Adults know... or learn... that life is full of moths, caterpillars, and worms.

(Pause)

But when I'm alone... fear sets in. I wonder... do I really want to be alone? Maybe their visits comfort me.

(She seems to see someone else)

Was it you that touched me that day?

(Sadly)

And if you are still here, why do I feel so alone?

(Sees Doctor again and gets upset, almost in a panic)

Please, stay away. She won't visit me if you're here. Please. Go!

(Turns back to the new person she sees)

Mother? Mother is that you?

(Sits up quickly - startled)

Mother!

(Breathing hard - cries - the person is gone - she calms down)

I'm sorry - I'm so sorry - There's usually no one to listen - at least no one who's willing to bend - Why are you still here? What's the use of talking if it doesn't do anyone any good?

(Sighs - doctor won't leave)

Do you believe in an afterlife? Like heaven and angels and pearly gates - free of all Earthly strife - I think it's a lot less defined than that - I think maybe we all end up a part of greater whole - a tiny molecule in a bigger being or a little star in a vast universe - we'll return to where we came from - whether it's God, the Great Spirit, or something else - but I know that's where we will be - Everything around me seems to point to the same conclusion - "ashes to ashes - dust to dust" - where we begin is where we end - the Earth gives us life through what we eat and we give her life when we die - the source is the finish - rain that feeds the river comes from the sea - to each beginning there is a definable end -

(She looks at the sky and smiles)

I know it's getting dark but I don't want to go back inside anymore - I don't like my room - this is where I want to stay -

(Looks at doctor)

You can't keep me caged any longer - The locked doors won't hold me anymore - Did you know I can fly?

(She looks up at the night sky)

I'm leaving all the Earthly matters to you - I belong near a different sun -

(Points to a star)

I wish I were that star over there - The little one next to Orion - that way I'd never be lonely - It's so free out there - no one can touch you or hurt you - you can simply shine - People don't like it when you shine - that's why stars are up there and not down here - humans think the brightness is offensive -

(Pause - looks and smiles at the stars)

My mother is a star now - She always seemed like one to me - but stars don't like it very well where they can't be stars anymore -

(Pause - grows sad)

I want to be a star - stars having meaning - stars I understand - Now those stars up there in the sky have staying power. I can always count on them. I can always look up and know they'll be there for me. The stars on Earth burn out too quickly. They have a moment where they shine so bright but then poof. They're gone. A memory. Sometimes not even that. But with the stars in the sky, I know they'll be there night after night, always there for me to make a wish.

I make wishes all the time. I watch for the first star each night and say...

"Star light star bright, first star I see tonight... I wish I may, I wish I might, have the wish I wish tonight..." I always make the same wish, but I can't tell you what it is. Then it might not come true. I really want it too. It would change my life.

I would always go to wishing wells with lucky pennies... Those pennies you find that people have lost... Unlucky for them... Lucky for me... Then I toss them in the wishing well in front of the old museum. And I toss them in the fountain at the park... Each time making my wish.

Have you ever wanted anything that badly in your life? So badly that you can't imagine your future without it?

I would be so sad if my life wasn't different... If things didn't change... If I was still stuck here... In this life. But I won't stop wishing... I can't...

I don't want to be left with nothing... I want some meaning... A reason things my life turned out this way. I want this suffering to be worthwhile.

END OF MONOLOGUE

SCENE 21 - SAFETY IN NUMBERS (MR. DAVIS)

Look. I know this sounds stupid but you need to ban together. There's safety in numbers. So we're going to start a club.

(Responds to something one of the students says)

No, it's not the losers club. The best way to stop being bullied and stop being victims is to find others like you and work together. You know, like watch out for each other. Bullies want to pick us off one by one but they avoid a group. They look for weak ones who stray from the herd and try to pick us off when we're alone, but if we stay strong and stay together, we can survive this.

Come on people. You came to me because you had a problem. You are picked on. You are victims. And this my answer. All of you can work together and turn things around.

We're going to be a club that helps others. We'll be the helpers instead of the hurters. We'll find ways we can make things better. We can pick up trash, do soup kitchens or help the homeless. We'll volunteer to help others in need. We'll go to elementary schools and read with kids. We'll help little kids who are bullied and patrol the playgrounds. Whatever good we can do, we'll do it.

Okay, okay. I'm getting carried away. We can't do everything. But I think it's important, not only to be here for each other, but to help other people too. So what do you say? Want to be in my club?

END OF MONOLOGUE

SCENE 22 - END THE HURTING

LUKE

When you're hurting you look for weakness.

LAYLA

You take that hurt and pass it on to me.

BING

You're hurting... so you hurt.

MOIRA

You're damaged... so you damage.

LANE

You're feeling pain so you cause pain... in me.

(The light becomes brighter and the face transforms looking stronger and determined)

LUKE

It has to stop.

LAYLA

I will protect myself from the pain.

BING

I know the damage must be undone.

MOIRA

I will end the hurting so I never hurt.

LANE

And I must do it... for me.

END OF MONOLOGUE

BONUS MONOLOGUES

STRONG ENOUGH FOR BOTH OF US

MOIRA

Yes, you're right. I have to toughen up… there's always someone who has it worse than me.

Sorry I am so depressed all the time… sorry I bring you down. I don't mean to ruin your day… Or your life.

I'd love to stop being depressed.

I wish I could look on the bright side and turn that frown upside down. I wish it were that easy.

You think it's my fault don't you? You think it's all in my head.

Yes, we all have this problem don't we? We all get a little blue sometimes. I get very blue all the time. I'm so blue I'm purple.

Don't tell me you understand… you don't understand!

Do you really know how this feels? Do you really know how this grips me inside and threatens to rip me apart? Do you know the weight that holds me down, a weight so powerful I can hardly move?

Yes, I'm using this to punish you. I am angry at you so I'm acting this way to hurt you…

I need to stop feeling sorry for myself… Me, me, me... yes, it's all about me… I want you all to drop everything and focus on me!

I'm sorry I even came out of my room.

Oh yeah… a nice cup of tea will instantly cure me - maybe if you put some strychnine in it.

I wish I could just snap out of it… like it was some kind of spell a witch cast on me. I'm waiting for some prince to come along and kiss my tears away.

Don't worry. I won't say anything anymore. I didn't want to bring it up. I didn't want to talk about it anyway…

I bet you're sorry you asked how I was doing.

How am I doing anyway?

I'm hurting so bad. I wish there was something that would take away the pain. I can't handle this much longer.

All I want to know is that I'm not alone… that I'm important to someone. Maybe I want a hug sometimes. Maybe I want someone to tell me I'm not going crazy, that's it's not really my fault. I need to know I didn't do this to myself and that I'm not the cause of this horrible thing that's happening to me. I want someone to be here for me and help me through this. I need someone stronger than me… I'm so weak. I need someone who is strong enough for both of us.

I need to know you'll be there for me… I need to know you'll never give up on me. That you'll never leave me. That you'll never go away. And I need someone to help me not give up on myself.

I want to know that I'm important. That I matter. That I'm loved. Tell me that things will get better.

It helps to have someone to talk to… it helps to say something… thank you for listening… thank you for not leaving me alone anymore.

END OF MONOLOGUE

The following are different versions of monologues in this play.

TEARING ME APART

JANEY

Now those stars up there in the sky have staying power. I can always count on them. I can always look up and know they'll be there for me. The stars on Earth burn out too quickly. They have a moment where they shine so bright but then poof. They're gone. A memory. Sometimes not even that. But with the stars in the sky, I know they'll be there night after night, always there for me to make a wish.

I make wishes all the time. I watch for the first star each night and say...

"Star light star bright, first star I see tonight... I wish I may, I wish I might, have the wish I wish tonight..." I always make the same wish, but I can't tell you what it is. Then it might not come true. I really want it too. It would change my life.

So I go to wishing wells with lucky pennies... Those pennies you find that people have lost... Unlucky for them... Lucky for me... Then I toss them in the wishing well in front of the old museum. And I toss them in the fountain at the mall... Each time making my wish.

Have you ever wanted anything that badly in your life? So badly that you can't imagine your future without it?

I would be so sad if my life wasn't different... If things didn't change... If I was still stuck here... In this life. But I won't stop wishing... I can't...

I don't want to be left with nothing... I want some meaning... A reason things my life turned out this way. I want this suffering to be worthwhile.

I suffer every day and you don't even see it. You don't see the hurt inside me do you? But it's too much to hold inside anymore.

I can't handle it... I'm going crazy. The fear is crippling me... I have to drag myself out of bed and force myself to live each day... Sure, I put on this happy face... I bet you think I am pretty cheerful... No one cares to see the pain under my skin... The pain that's ripping at me... And tearing me apart.

END

SHADOWS OF THE PAST

(Janey is in a garden watching the stars in the sky. She becomes upset when someone approaches)

JANEY

I was hoping I could be alone out here in the garden. No one ever comes here in the evening. I wanted to be here for the stars.

 (Angrily)

I don't want anything - and I don't want to talk anymore - can I please be by myself? That's all you've done here - poke, prop, and pry - I've never felt so violated before - I just want to be left alone.

(Pause)

I don't like being around anyone. I get upset when I'm in a room full of people.

 (Pause... afraid)

I get really scared - I almost feel like I can't breathe - I just need to be alone, Doctor - I know you don't really care - you're simply doing your job - once I'm "better" you'll be though with me - then it's on to another patient - you're just like anyone else -

(Almost shouting)
   You probably haven't cared about any patient in years - that would be unprofessional - an unnecessary burden on your conscience - Please, just go - I know what I need better than you -

You're not God, you know - you don't have the powers to cure everything - I know what you can and can't do -Go on - get out of here!

(Pause - she gets an evil smile)

Relax?

(Laughs)

How can I relax with you bothering me all the time? If there's another way, I'd like to know how -

(Pause. Turns away)

Is there anything else you wish to pry out of me? No? Good - then goodnight -

(JANEY starts weeding the flower bed)

I thought you were leaving - Sorry but I'm busy - I'm killing weeds - Cultivating beauty by killing the ugly - it's an odd practice - in reality its weeds on which the soil feeds -

(Stops)

But few people find the truth as fulfilling - If only you had planted something more useful - beans, or tomatoes, then the sacrifice might be worthwhile - but flowers, they're more difficult to justify - Frail beauty - that's all they are - cultivated for weakness - and has very little nutritional value - in the end they never can satisfy - always a disappointment as they wither and die - Frail and weak - a light frost would snap its neck -

(JANEY breaks the head off a flower)

So easily smitten by one little insect -

(JANEY holds up broken bud to a weed)

The choice is so easy for most - Yet it's not - I suppose most people don't give it much thought -

(Looks up at sky)

I know a story of a man who had a plant which most called a useless weed - it turned out the weed was a cure for cancer - but the weed was nearly extinct so no one got the cure - do you believe in such a thing? Do you believe in anything?

(Pause)

Oh, never mind - I guess to you most beliefs are only fables -

(Throws both plants down - upset)

No one really cares, do they? They pay you to care - everywhere it's the same way - People should only fix what's broken - Why couldn't you all just leave me alone? Nothing was wrong with me before you found me - I was happy at home - alone - shut out from then world - protected -

(Pause. Calms a moment. Grows sadder)

I had to be alone - I - I needed to hide - I had no choice - I had to get away - I couldn't live like the others anymore -

(Angry)

Why do you want to know all this?

(Furious)

I said I don't want to talk anymore! Leave me alone! I don't have to tell you anything! I'm not a little kid.

(Bends over and buries her face in her hands)

There's so much you don't know - I just need to be alone - Why can't they leave me alone?

(She sees something)

But I'm never alone - There's always someone - Or something - Around me - Following me - They're always near - Spirits - Ghosts - Shadows of the past - Ghosts have always been with me. Not by choice. At least not on my part. It just happens. I don't want to believe... but they've forced themselves on me.

(Thoughtful)

Perhaps the old Indian woman did it to me. I lived in her house too long as a child.

(Looks at ceiling)

At night, footsteps paced the ceiling. Over and over, an impatient march, forever in step to a silent drum. If only this had been my only encounter, I could dismiss it. "The house is settling," my mother said... but this wasn't all the house did. Lights dimmed and glowed. Her ghostly will stronger than the new world magic conjured by GE. I slept in my room. Well, not really slept. Sleep was never something I did much of, especially early on. My worries at seven far outweighed my need for sleep. Awake. Forever awake. My father had left me. My mother... I was always worried mother would leave me too. I wish the ghosts would go. But they linger. Always lingering. Never really gone. The old Indian woman was my first. She rocked at my beside, all in white. My eyes met hers. Her eyes giving me a worried look as if I were the one who had expired. Fear making my head sink deeply into covers. My eyes entombed by my lids. How long she waited, I'll never know. By dawn I ventured a look. She was gone... or perhaps she was never there. Thinking the apparition a dream, I told my family and their eyes betrayed them. Others had known her too. Mother had a vision. She did not go questing for it though. The old Indian, young to most who saw her, once lived on this land. A servant. A girl died here, she at her side... at her side rocking... and the girl died. I wish I could have been there for her too... Spirits dog me. Just when I no longer believe, they appear. Flashing white lights. A cold touch. They return. Even now. But this time it was too much. Another place. Another spirit. This time it was someone I knew.

(Slowly turns to panic during following)

It started with the call. The news that she had gone away. Finding myself in tears. Tears sapping me dry. Would the tears ever stop? Pain like a thick metal pole shoved up your ass.

(Tries to calm herself but panics again)

I had lost everything. An emptiness replaced love, anxious to find, nothing there... no body anyway, but something. Something that opens doors, something leaving tissue by the bed. The dog barking at nothing... but something. Finding things in new places, things missing. The locked door... open.

(Tries to calm herself)

Explanations fly. Knowledge our protection.

(Thinks a moment. Frowns and shivers)

It began with the cold. Spots of cold. A moment of normal then cold, as if the heat were sucked into another dimension. These don't bother me as much as the touch. A handless touch of nothing. Something grabbed by arm but no one was there.

(Pulls back in fear and runs. She falls to the ground)

I ran for bed, buried myself in covers and waited for dawn.

(She curls up in a ball. Pause)

You're never too old to hide under the covers. Wrapping yourself up into a cocoon. Hoping that when you emerge life will be butterflies again.

(She sighs and sits up)

But only children believe in butterflies.

(She rises again)

Adults know... or learn... that life is full of moths, caterpillars, and worms.

(Pause)

But when I'm alone... fear sets in. I wonder... do I really want to be alone? Maybe their visits comfort me.
    (She seems to see someone else)

Was it you that touched me that day?

(Sadly)

And if you are still here, why do I feel so alone?

(Sees Doctor again and gets upset, almost in a panic)

Please, stay away. She won't visit me if you're here. Please. Go!

(Turns back to the new person she sees)
    Mother? Mother is that you?

(Sits up quickly - startled)

Mother!

(Breathing hard - cries - the person is gone - she calms down)

I'm sorry - I'm so sorry - There's usually no one to listen - at least no one who's willing to bend - Why are you still here? What's the use of talking if it doesn't do anyone any good?

(Sighs - doctor won't leave)

Do you believe in an afterlife? Like heaven and angels and pearly gates
- free of all Earthly strife - I think it's a lot less defined than that - I think
maybe we all end up a part of greater whole - a tiny molecule in a bigger
being or a little star in a vast universe - we'll return to where we came
from - whether it's God, the Great Spirit, or something else - but I know
that's where we will be - Everything around me seems to point to the
same conclusion - "ashes to ashes - dust to dust" - where we begin is
where we end - the Earth gives us life through what we eat and we give
her life when we die - the source is the finish - rain that feeds the river
comes from the sea - to each beginning there is a definable end -

(She looks at the sky and smiles)

I know it's getting dark but I don't want to go back inside anymore - I
don't like my room - this is where I want to stay -

(Looks at doctor)

You can't keep me caged any longer - The locked doors won't hold me
anymore - Did you know I can fly?

(She looks up at the night sky)

I'm leaving all the Earthly matters to you - I belong near a different sun -

(Points to a star)

I wish I were that star over there - The little one next to Orion - that way
I'd never be lonely - It's so free out there - no one can touch you or hurt
you - you can simply shine - People don't like it when you shine - that's
why stars are up there and not down here - humans think the brightness
is offensive -

(Pause - looks and smiles at the stars)

My mother is a star now - She always seemed like one to me - but stars
don't like it very well where they can't be stars anymore -

(Pause – grows sad)

I want to be a star – stars having meaning – stars I understand – Now
those stars up there in the sky have staying power. I can always count

on them. I can always look up and know they'll be there for me. The stars on Earth burn out too quickly. They have a moment where they shine so bright but then poof. They're gone. A memory. Sometimes not even that. But with the stars in the sky, I know they'll be there night after night, always there for me to make a wish.

I make wishes all the time. I watch for the first star each night and say...

"Star light star bright, first star I see tonight... I wish I may, I wish I might, have the wish I wish tonight..." I always make the same wish, but I can't tell you what it is. Then it might not come true. I really want it too. It would change my life.

I would always go to wishing wells with lucky pennies... Those pennies you find that people have lost... Unlucky for them... Lucky for me... Then I toss them in the wishing well in front of the old museum. And I toss them in the fountain at the park... Each time making my wish.

Have you ever wanted anything that badly in your life? So badly that you can't imagine your future without it?

I would be so sad if my life wasn't different... If things didn't change... If I was still stuck here... In this life. But I won't stop wishing... I can't...

I don't want to be left with nothing... I want some meaning... A reason things my life turned out this way. I want this suffering to be worthwhile.

END OF MONOLOGUE

48

WISHING STAR

JANEY

Now those stars up there in the sky have staying power. I can always count on them. I can always look up and know they'll be there for me. The stars on Earth burn out too quickly. They have a moment where they shine so bright but then poof. They're gone. A memory. Sometimes not even that. But with the stars in the sky, I know they'll be there night after night, always there for me to make a wish.

I make wishes all the time. I watch for the first star each night and say...

"Star light star bright, first star I see tonight... I wish I may, I wish I might, have the wish I wish tonight..." I always make the same wish, but I can't tell you what it is. Then it might not come true. I really want it too. It would change my life.

So I go to wishing wells with lucky pennies... Those pennies you find that people have lost... Unlucky for them... Lucky for me... Then I toss them in the wishing well in front of the old museum. And I toss them in the fountain at the mall... Each time making my wish.

Have you ever wanted anything that badly in your life? So badly that you can't imagine your future without it?

I would be so sad if my life wasn't different... If things didn't change... If I was still stuck here... In this life. But I won't stop wishing... I can't...

I don't want to be left with nothing... I want some meaning... A reason things my life turned out this way. I want this suffering to be worthwhile.

END OF MONOLOGUE

DOUBLE RAINBOW

LAYLA

I live for rainbows. They are magical. I love how they surprise you.

They can happen anywhere and at any time. Sometimes they're only there for a few seconds but I could watch them for hours.

And you know what's great about them ... Anyone can enjoy a rainbow... Rich, poor, famous, homeless, popular or loser. Anyone can see them and dream.

The time they dazzle me the most is after a terrible storm. Lightening terrifies me but rainbows bring me comfort again.

Oh! Oh! Look! Lookie! It's a double rainbow!! It's really a double ray... ay... ay... bbbb... boooooow! Thank you rainbows! Thank you!

I'm in Heaven.

END OF MONOLOGUE

MUCH MADNESS

JANEY
I want to be alone - I can't be around other people -

(Pause. Looks up, afraid)

I get really scared - I almost feel like I can't breathe -

(Panics a little)

I just need to be alone, Doctor -

(Angry)

You don't really care - you're simply doing your job - once I'm "better"
you'll be through with me - then it's on to another person -

(Gives a mean look)

You're just like everyone else -

(Speaking viciously)

- you probably haven't cared about anyone in years - that would be
unprofessional - and a burden you don't need for yourself -

(She pauses. Calms a little)

Please, just let me go - I know what I need better than you -

(Angry again)

You're not God, you know - you don't have the powers to cure everything
- I know what you can and can't do -

(Screams)

Go on - get out now!

(Long pause and silence. Cries)

No one really cares, do they -

(Struggles to talk through her tears)

You think you can help me - change me -

(Pause)

People should only fix what's broken -

(Furious)

I said I don't want to talk anymore! Leave me alone! I don't have to tell you anything! I'm not a little kid.

(Bends over and buries her face in her hands. Cries for a bit and then is much calmer)

There's so much you don't know -

(She looks up at the sky)

- if only I could fly -

(Her eyes look in wonder)

I'm leaving all the Earthly matters to you - I belong near a different sun -

(Points to a star)

I wish I were a star - part of some constellation so I would never be lonely.

- it's so free out there - no one can touch you or hurt you - you can simply shine -

(Pauses)

People don't like it when you shine - that's why stars are up there and not down here - humans think the brightness is offensive -

(Pause - looks and smiles at the stars)

My mother is a star now -

She always seemed like one to me - but stars don't like it very well where they can't be stars anymore - so they fade away - never shining again -

(Pause - grows sad)

I want to be a star - stars having meaning - stars I understand -

END OF MONOLOGUE

Made in the USA
San Bernardino, CA
03 March 2017